STRUCTURAL WONDERS OF THE WORLD

SUEZ CANAL

JOY GREGORY

www.av2books.com

AV² provides enriched content that supplements and complements this book. Weigl's AV² books strive to create inspired learning and engage young minds in a total learning experience.

Your AV² Media Enhanced books come alive with...

Audio
Listen to sections of the book read aloud.

Key Words
Study vocabulary, and complete a matching word activity.

Video
Watch informative video clips.

Quizzes
Test your knowledge.

Embedded Weblinks
Gain additional information for research.

Slideshow
View images and captions, and prepare a presentation.

Try This!
Complete activities and hands-on experiments.

... and much, much more!

Go to **www.av2books.com**, and enter this book's unique code.

BOOK CODE

AVE36366

AV² by Weigl brings you media enhanced books that support active learning.

Published by AV² by Weigl
350 5th Avenue, 59th Floor
New York, NY 10118
Website: www.av2books.com

Library of Congress Control Number: 2019934073

ISBN 978-1-7911-0590-7 (hardcover)
ISBN 978-1-7911-0591-4 (softcover)
ISBN 978-1-7911-0592-1 (multi-user eBook)
ISBN 978-1-7911-0593-8 (single user eBook)

Printed in Guangzhou, China
1 2 3 4 5 6 7 8 9 0   23 22 21 20 19

022019
103118

Project Coordinator: Heather Kissock
Art Director: Terry Paulhus
Layout: Ana María Vidal

Photo Credits
Every reasonable effort has been made to trace ownership and to obtain permission to reprint copyright material. The publishers would be pleased to have any errors or omissions brought to their attention so that they may be corrected in subsequent printings.

Weigl acknowledges Getty Images, Alamy, Newscom, Bridgeman Images, iStock, Shutterstock, and Dreamstime as its primary image suppliers for this title.

SUEZ CANAL

Contents

Introducing the Suez Canal

The Suez Canal was designed to improve international trade.

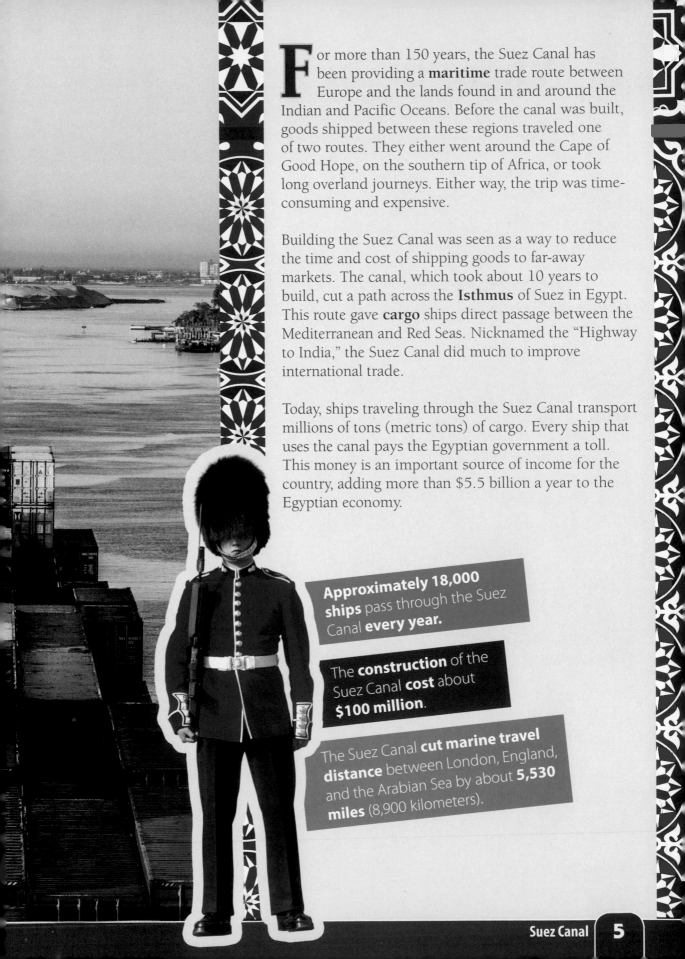

For more than 150 years, the Suez Canal has been providing a **maritime** trade route between Europe and the lands found in and around the Indian and Pacific Oceans. Before the canal was built, goods shipped between these regions traveled one of two routes. They either went around the Cape of Good Hope, on the southern tip of Africa, or took long overland journeys. Either way, the trip was time-consuming and expensive.

Building the Suez Canal was seen as a way to reduce the time and cost of shipping goods to far-away markets. The canal, which took about 10 years to build, cut a path across the **Isthmus** of Suez in Egypt. This route gave **cargo** ships direct passage between the Mediterranean and Red Seas. Nicknamed the "Highway to India," the Suez Canal did much to improve international trade.

Today, ships traveling through the Suez Canal transport millions of tons (metric tons) of cargo. Every ship that uses the canal pays the Egyptian government a toll. This money is an important source of income for the country, adding more than $5.5 billion a year to the Egyptian economy.

Approximately 18,000 **ships** pass through the Suez Canal **every year.**

The **construction** of the Suez Canal **cost** about **$100 million**.

The Suez Canal **cut marine travel distance** between London, England, and the Arabian Sea by about **5,530 miles** (8,900 kilometers).

Where Is the Suez Canal?

The Isthmus of Suez is the only land bridge between Africa and Asia. Spanning about 75 miles (121 km), it serves as the boundary between the two continents. The Suez Canal runs in a north–south direction across the isthmus. To its west is the low-lying Nile River **delta**. To the east, at a higher **elevation**, lies the Sinai **Peninsula**.

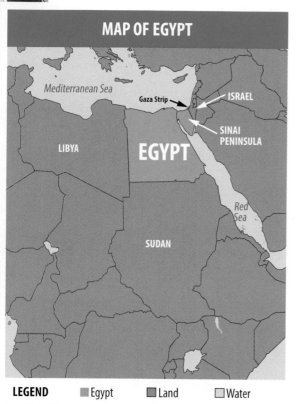

MAP OF EGYPT

Mediterranean Sea

Gaza Strip

ISRAEL

SINAI PENINSULA

LIBYA

EGYPT

Red Sea

SUDAN

LEGEND ■ Egypt ■ Land □ Water

Depth
The Suez Canal has a maximum depth of 79 feet (24 meters).

Egypt is a country in the **Middle East**. Its northern border follows the shoreline of the Mediterranean Sea. The African countries of Libya and Sudan are on the western and southern borders of Egypt. Israel, which is part of the continent of Asia, borders the northeast part of the country. The Red Sea forms the country's eastern border.

The Suez Canal was built in the late 1800s. Parts of the canal follow a route dug thousands of years earlier. Known as the Canal of the **Pharaohs**, this original canal was used to move goods between the Red Sea and the Nile River.

Today, the canal links the Egyptian cities of Suez and **Port** Said. Suez lies at the south end of the canal. Port Said sits at the north. As ships move along the canal, they travel through several Egyptian lakes. The waters of Lake Manzala, Lake Timsah, Little Bitter Lake, and Great Bitter Lake are all connected by the Suez Canal.

Length
The Suez Canal is 120 miles (193 km) long.

79 feet
(24 m)

120 miles
(193 km)

Width
At its surface, the canal is 1,027 feet (313 m) wide. Below the surface, the canal's width ranges from 397 to 738 feet (121 to 225 m).

1,027 feet
(313 m)

Building the Suez Canal

Poor Egyptians were forced to work for the Suez Canal Company. They toiled long hours and received low wages.

France and Egypt were the two countries responsible for initiating the construction of the Suez Canal. The actual work was done by the Suez Canal Company. At first, the canal was dug by hand under difficult working conditions. Many workers died due to disease and the heat. Working conditions improved when the Suez Canal Company brought machines to the work site. Those machines handled most of the 98 million cubic yards (75 million cubic meters) of earth and sand that were moved to build the canal.

When the canal opened, ships could move only one way at a time. Passing bays were soon built. They allowed ships to pull to the side so other ships could move past them. Several lakes also served as passing lanes. Today, the Suez Canal offers two-way traffic for large ships. Many of the ships traveling north carry oil products. Vessels traveling south often carry grain and fertilizer from North America and Europe.

Canal upgrades began in 2014. By 2023, approximately 97 ships are expected to travel the Suez Canal each day. That will be nearly double the number that used the canal in 2014.

Timeline

About 1830 BC
Egyptian Pharaoh Senusret III oversees construction of a canal to move goods between the Nile River and the Red Sea. The canal is later filled in for military reasons.

1858 AD
The Suez Canal Company is established to build a canal across the Isthmus of Suez.

1869
Construction of the Suez Canal finishes. The canal opens for business.

1876
Upgrades begin to make the Suez Canal wider and deeper. This allows more and larger ships to use the passage.

1956
Egypt **nationalizes** the canal. This leads to the Suez Crisis, a brief war between Egypt and the United Kingdom, France, and Israel.

1882
The United Kingdom invades Egypt, and the canal is placed under British control.

1967–1975
Egypt and Israel are at war. The canal is closed to traffic.

2014
The president of Egypt announces a multi-billion-dollar project for canal improvements. The upgrades include wider and deeper lanes for two-way traffic and larger ships.

2019
The 150th anniversary of the opening of the Suez Canal is celebrated.

The Structure of the Suez Canal

The Suez Canal connects two shipping ports that are located at almost the same elevation. This allowed builders to construct the Suez Canal as a sea-level shipping route. The canal did not require the addition of **locks**, a feature found in many of the world's other canals.

ENTRANCES Ships entering the Suez Canal on either end do so through **dredged** approach channels. There are two channels at Port Said and one at Suez. The Port Said entrance also has two long **breakwaters**. These were built to protect the canal from **silt** buildup caused by strong coastal currents.

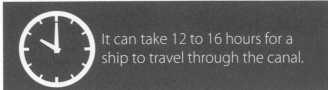
It can take 12 to 16 hours for a ship to travel through the canal.

SHIPPING LANES In 2015, Egypt finished an $8.5-billion upgrade to the Suez Canal. The project added 22 miles (35 km) of new shipping channels. Another 23 miles (37 km) of existing canal were dredged to allow larger ships. The work decreased the time ships need to wait to pass each other. Travel times have improved, and more ships can now use the canal at the same time.

BENDS The Suez Canal does not take the shortest route across the Isthmus of Suez. Instead of a straight passage across the isthmus, the canal has eight bends. These bends allow ships to make use of four lakes located on the isthmus. The bends add about 45 miles (72 km) to the canal route.

More than 9 billion cubic feet (258 million cubic m) of earth and sand were removed to add new channels to the Suez Canal.

The increased canal traffic brought by the upgrades is expected to generate $13 billion in shipping tolls by 2023.

Suez Canal Features

The Suez Canal is a transportation hub. While ships traverse the waters, other types of vehicles also make use of the canal. Conduits have been built to allow cars, trucks, and trains to travel both over and under the canal. This enables the transfer of even more goods and people.

AHMED HAMDI TUNNEL People can drive under the Suez Canal by way of the Ahmed Hamdi Tunnel. Built in 1983 by the British government, the tunnel is 1.01 miles (1.63 km) long and reaches a depth of 167 feet (51 m) below ground. The tunnel's two lanes allow traffic to move in opposite directions at the same time.

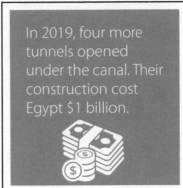

In 2019, four more tunnels opened under the canal. Their construction cost Egypt $1 billion.

AL-FERDAN RAILWAY BRIDGE The Al-Ferdan Railway Bridge is the longest rotating metal bridge in the world. It is made up of two arms, one on each side of the canal, and two 10-foot (3-m) wide lanes for high-speed traffic. Prior to the 2015 upgrades, the bridge allowed for the transport of goods from Egypt to the Sinai Peninsula. If a train needed to cross the canal, the arms would rotate from the canal's banks to join over the water. Today, the bridge is not in use, as there is no crossing over the new canal lane that was built.

When joined, the Al-Ferdan Railway Bridge has a span of 1,100 feet (335 m).

The Suez Canal Bridge is also known as the Egyptian-Japanese Friendship Bridge. Japan funded 60 percent of the bridge's construction.

SUEZ CANAL BRIDGE Opened in 2001, the Suez Canal Bridge was built to allow road traffic to cross the canal. The bridge is located at the northern end of the canal, near the town of El Qantara. It is 5.6 miles (9 km) long, including the two approaches on each side. The bridge is supported by cables that stretch from the two **pylons**. Each pylon is 505 feet (154 m) tall. The bridge's height gives it a 230-foot (70-m) clearance over the canal.

The Grand Design

A great deal of planning went into the construction of the Suez Canal. Designers knew international markets wanted a canal that would handle large ships. They also knew the structure had to stand the test of time.

Stability and Slope

Much of the Suez Canal is built from clay and sand. Sand is a very difficult material to stabilize. Without support, it shifts and moves into empty spaces. Clay, on the other hand, is slippery when wet, but hard when it dries. To ensure that the sand stayed secure, the builders used clay as a support. They strengthened the walls of the canal by stacking clay on the edge. After it dried in the sun, the clay stabilized the banks. Extra stability was added by building the walls of the canal at a 2:1 slope. This means that the top of the canal is twice as wide as the bottom. This slope stabilized the sides of the canal and helped prevent its collapse.

Deadweight Tonnage

The people who built the Suez Canal had to consider the size of the ships that would pass through it. While the width of the ships was important, the **deadweight tonnage (DWT)** was also critical. DWT includes the **ballast**, cargo, fuel, passengers, crew, and supplies. If a ship's DWT is too high for a canal's design, the ship will not be able to move through the canal without scraping or getting stuck on the bottom. Ships in the Suez Canal can be no longer than 900 feet (274 m) long. They must have a DWT of 200,000 or less. This sizing designation is called Suezmax.

The Science Behind the Suez Canal

Until 1863, much of the Suez Canal was built by workers with hand tools. The construction went faster after the Suez Canal Company brought in machines to do the heavy work.

Steam Engines

The Suez Canal Company used steam-powered machines to dig and dredge much of the channel. This equipment could move 25 times as much earth in a day as a person could using hand tools. The operation of the engines relied on a system that used water and **pistons**. Water was heated in large boilers, which created steam. The steam expanded and compressed in the engine, causing the piston to move. The piston was connected to the moving parts of the machine. Its movement made the machine run.

Grade Rods

The people who built the Suez Canal used grade rods to guide the placement of sand and earth. Grade rods are marked with different measurements, called graduations. The graduations can be in feet or inches, meters or centimeters, or in fractions. The rods helped workers calculate the height and slope of the Suez Canal's walls. This allowed builders to make sure the canal was deep enough for large ships to pass through.

The Builders

The people who planned the Suez Canal foresaw the growth of the global shipping trade. Where others saw a dry piece of land, they envisioned a waterway that would change history.

Ferdinand de Lesseps Diplomat

Ferdinand de Lesseps was a French **diplomat** who worked in Egypt. There, he looked for ways to increase trade between western Europe, Asia, and Africa. De Lesseps, who was not an engineer, oversaw the construction of the Suez Canal. He was later hired to oversee construction of the Panama Canal. That canal was to be built across the isthmus that connects Central and South America. Work on the Panama Canal began in 1881, but de Lesseps was dismissed before it was built. A French court found de Lesseps and his son guilty of mismanaging the project. De Lesseps avoided jail but was heavily fined. His son spent a year in prison. De Lesseps died in France on December 7, 1894.

Said Pasha
Viceroy of Egypt

Said Pasha was the **viceroy** of Egypt from 1854 to 1863. The son of another viceroy, Said was a long-time friend of Ferdinand de Lesseps. Together, Said and de Lesseps supported construction of the Suez Canal. Later, Said and other Egyptian leaders opposed the project, but work continued without their support.

Alois Negrelli Engineer

Alois Negrelli was the civil engineer responsible for designing the Suez Canal. Born in 1799 in what is now the Italian province of Trentino, Negrelli received his schooling in Italy and Austria. His career began when he took a position working for Austria's Department of Construction. Negrelli later moved to Switzerland, where he built the first Swiss railroad between Zurich and Baden. He also oversaw construction of the Münster Bridge, a stone bridge built in Zurich. After working in Egypt, Negrelli lived in the Austrian Empire, where he designed buildings, railways, and telegraph lines.

Civil Engineers

The Suez Canal was designed by a civil engineer. This type of engineer is trained to design and develop **infrastructure** projects, such as roads and buildings. Civil engineers also play an important role in rebuilding projects, helping with reconstruction efforts following a natural disaster, for instance. Some civil engineers specialize in specific areas, such as environmental projects or marine-based structures.

Dredge Operators

Much of the canal's excavation was done using machines called dredgers. The safe operation of these machines required skilled workers. Today, dredge operators are in demand around the world. In fact, the Suez Canal still requires regular dredging, to clean up rocks and sand that have fallen into the water. Dredge operators make use of two types of dredgers to do the job. Mechanical dredgers use a giant bucket to scoop up rocks and sand. Hydraulic dredgers do the same thing using a vacuum effect.

Laborers

Many of the people who worked on the Suez Canal project were unskilled laborers. These laborers used picks and shovels to dig the canal bed. They then loaded the earth and sand into crates, which were carried to dump sites on camels. Laborers continued to work on the canal even after powered machines were brought to the site. Today, laborers continue to play an important role in construction. They perform many jobs, including cleaning sites, loading materials, and operating equipment.

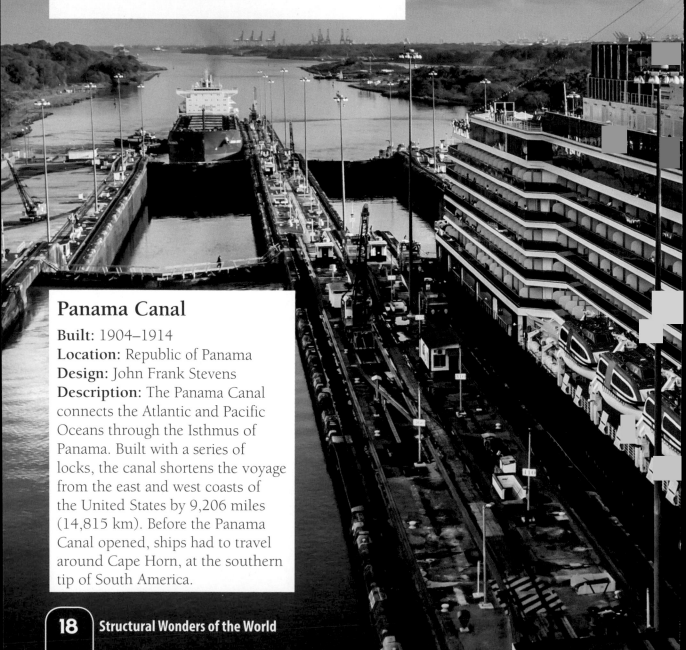

Similar Structures

People have been building canals for thousands of years. The first canals were built to control the flow of rivers and to transport goods short distances. Today, canals can be found in many parts of the world. Some canals still cover short distances. Others cross entire countries.

Panama Canal

Built: 1904–1914
Location: Republic of Panama
Design: John Frank Stevens
Description: The Panama Canal connects the Atlantic and Pacific Oceans through the Isthmus of Panama. Built with a series of locks, the canal shortens the voyage from the east and west coasts of the United States by 9,206 miles (14,815 km). Before the Panama Canal opened, ships had to travel around Cape Horn, at the southern tip of South America.

Beijing-Hangzhou Grand Canal

Built: 468 BC–607 AD
Location: China
Design: Fuchai and other emperors
Description: The Beijing-Hangzhou Grand Canal is the oldest and longest artificial canal in the world. The Grand Canal is 1,115 miles (1,794 km) long. It includes five rivers and connects four Chinese provinces. The canal was built to transport agricultural products to cities and armies. It was upgraded in the 1900s to accommodate larger boats.

Main-Danube Canal

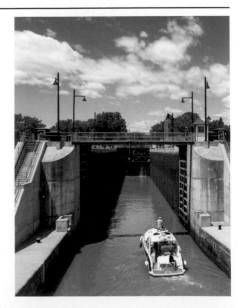

Built: 1960–1992
Location: Bavaria, Germany
Design: Rhein-Main-Donau AG (RMD)
Description: The Main-Danube Canal replaced one used before World War II. The updated version is 106 miles (171 km) long. It connects the North and Black Seas. This creates a waterway that spans 2,200 miles (3,541 km) through 15 countries. The canal's 16 locks raise ships 1,332 feet (406 m). This allows the ships to travel through the Swabian Alps, located south of Nürnberg, Germany.

Erie Canal

Built: 1817–1825
Location: New York State, United States
Design: DeWitt Clinton and Benjamin Wright
Description: The Erie Canal connects the Great Lakes with New York City through the Hudson River at Albany. The canal cuts through the Appalachian Mountains and is 363 miles (584 km) long. It was the first U.S. canal to connect western rivers with the Atlantic Ocean. Many of the engineers who helped build the Erie Canal used that experience to build other canals in the United States.

At Issue

The Suez Canal has done much to improve world trade. However, with its success have come problems. Joining two waterways caused environmental changes that could not have been predicted. As well, the importance of the canal has made it a target in times of conflict.

WHAT IS THE ISSUE?

About 350 non-**indigenous** species have entered the Mediterranean Sea since the Suez Canal opened.

Terrorists and countries engaged in conflicts have attempted to stage attacks on the Suez Canal and the ships that use it.

EFFECTS

These species endanger the native plants and animals in the sea. Their presence also puts some industries at risk.

In the summer of 2013, two ships in the canal were hit by rocket-propelled grenades.

ACTION TAKEN

Scientists are campaigning the United Nations and the Egyptian government for an environmental impact study. This study would assess the scope of the problem and help develop solutions.

Protective walls are being built along the northern and southern entrances to the canal. The Egyptian military has increased its presence along the canal route as well.

Activity

Water Displacement in Canals

Boats **displace** water. The heavier a boat is, the more water it displaces. Shipping companies must ensure that their boats can navigate a canal without getting stuck. They also have to make sure that the weight of their ships will not harm the canal itself. Try this experiment to find out more about the impact of water displacement.

Materials

A baking sheet

2 transparent or semi-transparent plastic containers, one small enough to float in the other

Felt pen

Water

Small rocks or pebbles

Ruler

Instructions

1. Fill the large container with water to create a model canal. Place it on top of the baking sheet to manage splashing.

2. Use the ruler and felt pen to mark the water level in the canal.

3. Place the smaller container, or boat, in the canal. Use the felt pen to mark the water level on the side of the boat.

4. Add some rocks, or cargo, to the boat. Use the felt pen to mark the new water level on the side of boat. Did the extra weight make the boat sit higher or lower in the water?

5. Look at the water level mark recorded on the side of your canal. How did the addition of weight to the boat affect the canal's water level?

6. Experiment with adding more rocks to the boat, or adding more boats to the canal, with or without rocks. How does this impact the water level of the canal?

8 Ways to Test Your Knowledge

1
Which two seas are connected by the Suez Canal?

3
Who oversaw the canal's construction?

2
How long is the Suez Canal?

4
What is the Suez Canal's nickname?

5
How many ships pass through the Suez Canal each year?

6
When did the Suez Canal open for business?

7
How long does it take for a ship to travel through the Suez Canal?

8
What is the name of the Egyptian port city located at the north end of the Suez Canal?

Answers

1. The Mediterranean Sea and the Red Sea **2.** 120 miles (193 km) **3.** Ferdinand de Lesseps **4.** Highway to India **5.** Approximately 18,000 **6.** 1869 **7.** 12 to 16 hours **8.** Port Said

Key Words

ballast: a heavy substance, such as water or rock, placed in the bottom of a ship to improve stability and control

breakwaters: offshore barriers built to protect a harbor from the force of waves

cargo: goods carried in a ship, truck, or airplane

deadweight tonnage (DWT): a measure of how much weight a ship can carry

delta: an area of low, flat land where a river divides into several smaller rivers before flowing into the sea

diplomat: a person from one country who represents that country in another nation

displace: to force something out of its usual position

dredged: removed unwanted things from the bottom of a body of water

elevation: the height above sea level

indigenous: occurring naturally in a particular region or environment

infrastructure: the basic physical and organizational structures and facilities in a city, country, or other area

isthmus: a narrow strip of land that connects two other pieces of land

locks: enclosures in canals that have gates at each end and are used to raise or lower boats as they pass from level to level

maritime: of the sea

Middle East: the countries of southwestern Asia and northern Africa

nationalizes: puts control in the hands of the government

peninsula: a piece of land that is nearly surrounded by water

pharaohs: rulers of ancient Egypt

pistons: cylinders or metal discs that are part of an engine

port: town or city located in a harbor where ships pick up or drop off cargo

pylons: tall, tower-like structures

silt: sand or soil that is carried along by flowing water and then dropped in a channel or harbor

viceroy: the person who represents the king in a country or province

Index

Log on to www.av2books.com

AV² by Weigl brings you media enhanced books that support active learning. Go to www.av2books.com, and enter the special code found on page 2 of this book. You will gain access to enriched and enhanced content that supplements and complements this book. Content includes video, audio, weblinks, quizzes, a slideshow, and activities.

AV² Online Navigation

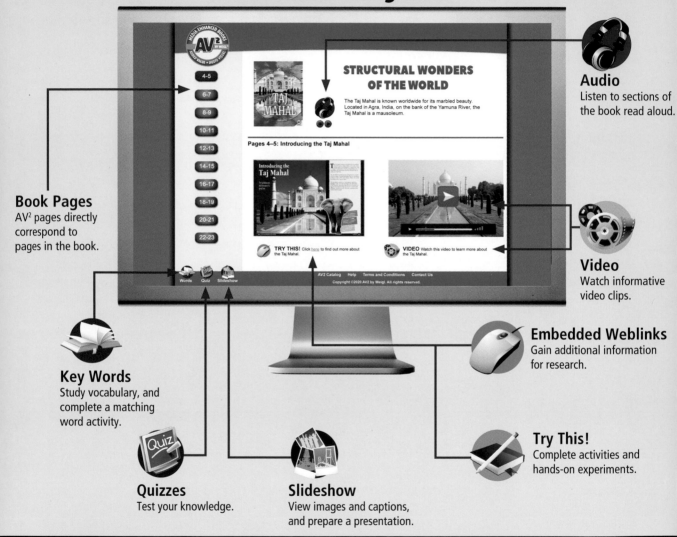

Book Pages
AV² pages directly correspond to pages in the book.

Audio
Listen to sections of the book read aloud.

Video
Watch informative video clips.

Key Words
Study vocabulary, and complete a matching word activity.

Quizzes
Test your knowledge.

Slideshow
View images and captions, and prepare a presentation.

Embedded Weblinks
Gain additional information for research.

Try This!
Complete activities and hands-on experiments.

AV² was built to bridge the gap between print and digital. We encourage you to tell us what you like and what you want to see in the future.

Sign up to be an AV² Ambassador at www.av2books.com/ambassador.

Due to the dynamic nature of the internet, some of the URLs and activities provided as part of AV² by Weigl may have changed or ceased to exist. AV² by Weigl accepts no responsibility for any such changes. All media enhanced books are regularly monitored to update addresses and sites in a timely manner. Contact AV² by Weigl at 1-866-649-3445 or av2books@weigl.com with any questions, comments, or feedback.